THE BEST

Black Sabbath

AMSCO PUBLICATIONS
New York/London/Sydney

Published by
Wise Publications
14-15 Berners Street, London W1T 3LJ, UK.

Exclusive Distributors:
Music Sales Corporation
180 Madison Avenue, 24th Floor, New York NY 10016, USA.
Music Sales Limited
Distribution Centre, Newmarket Road, Bury St Edmunds, Suffolk IP33 3YB, UK.
Music Sales Pty Limited
Units 3-4, 17 Willfox Street, Condell Park, NSW 2200, Australia.

Order No. AM928818
ISBN: 978-0-8256-1460-6
This book © Copyright 1996 by Amsco Publications,
a division of Music Sales Corporation, New York.

Front cover photograph: Steve Granitz/Retna Limited.
Back cover photograph: Jodi Summers Dorland/Retna Limited.

Printed in the EU.

Contents

Legend of Music Symbols

Black Sabbath

Words and Music by Frank Iommi, John Osbourne, William Ward, and Terence Butler

Play 3 times

*G5 = G (omit 3rd)

Changes

Words and Music by Frank Iommi, Terence Butler, William Ward, and John Osbourne

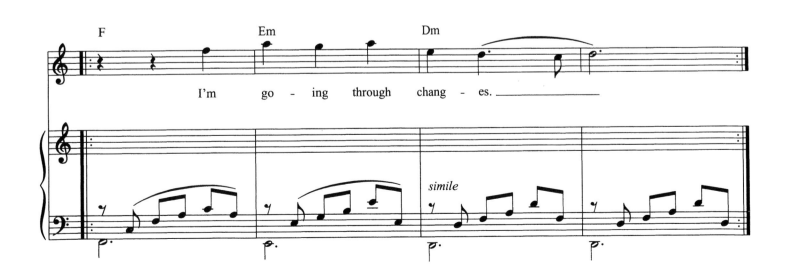

Children Of The Grabe

Words and Music by Frank Iommi, William Ward, John Osbourne, and Terence Butler

*To play along with recording, tune all strings down one whole step.
**C5 = C(omit 3rd)

have to live___ and all the hate that's in___ their hearts.___ They're
mor-row bring - ing peace in an - y way?___
place to live,___ then spread the word___ to - day.___

tired of be - ing pushed___ a - round___ and told___ just what___ to do.___
Must the world___ live in___ the shad - ow of___ a - tom - ic fear?___
Show the world___ that love___ is still___ a - live. You must___ be brave,___

To Coda I
Last time to Coda II

_____ They'll fight the world___ un - til___ they've won___ and
Can they win___ the fight___ for peace___ or
Or you chil - dren of___ to - day___ are

D.S. 𝄋 (no repeats, lyric 2) al Coda I

love comes flow - ing through.___

Guitar Fig. 4 (2 bars)

T
A
B

Coda I

Play Fig. 4

Em5
Play Fig. 2

will they dis - ap - pear?___

G5   C5   D5

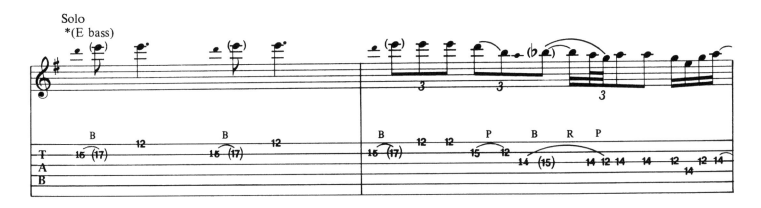

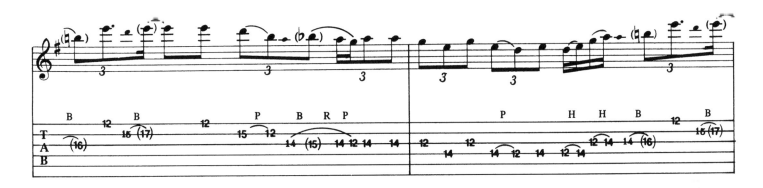

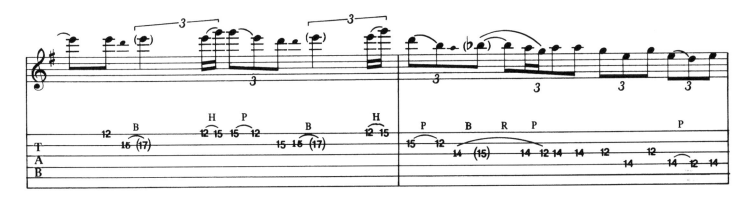

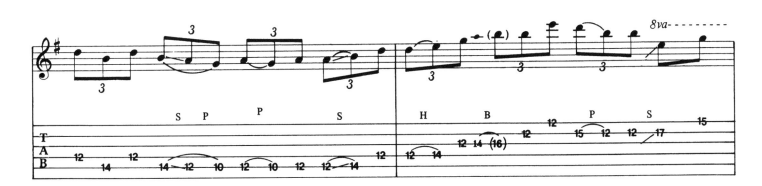

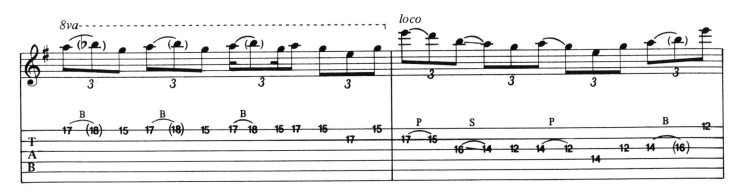

*Indicates note played by Bass Guitar only.

Play 3 times

Dirty Women

Words and Music by Frank Iommi, Terence Butler, William Ward, and John Osbourne

* Indicates note played by Bass Guitar only
** Right channel overdub not notated

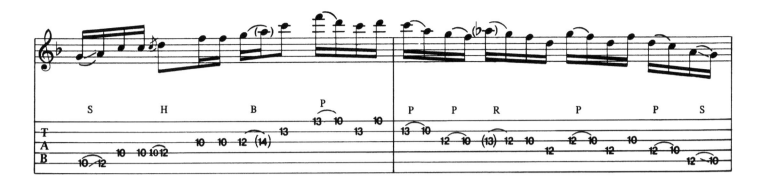

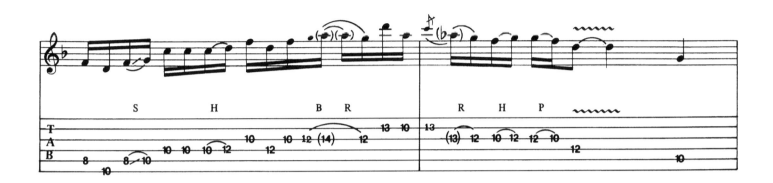

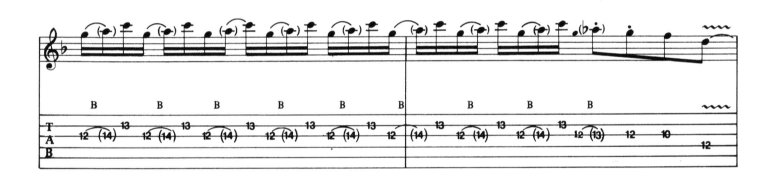

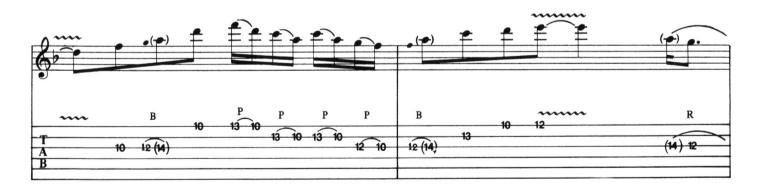

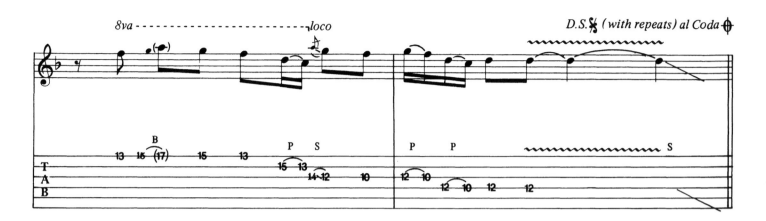

Play 4 times

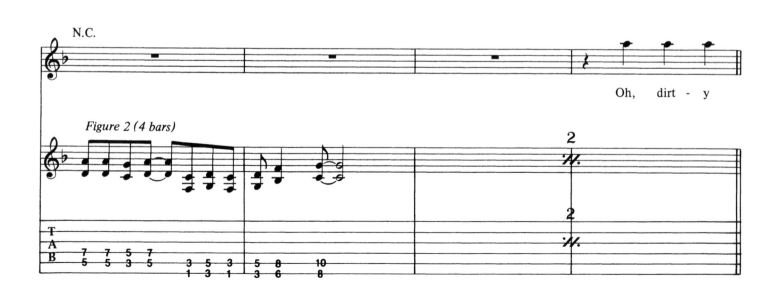

Looking For Today

Words and Music by Frank Iommi, William Ward, Terence Butler, and John Osbourne

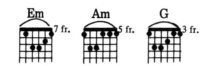

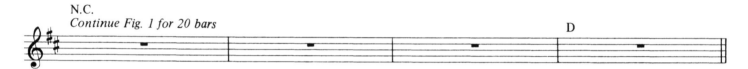

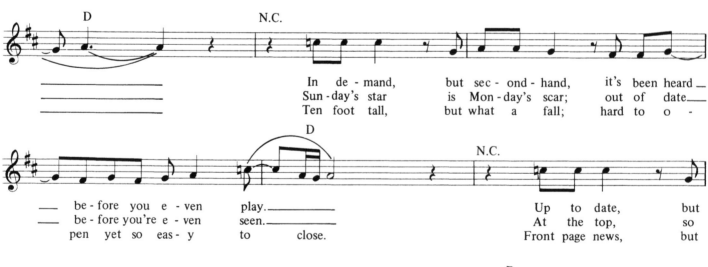

It's com-plete, but ob-so-lete. All to-mor-rows be-come yes-ter day.
Don't de-lay; you're in to-day, but to-mor-row is an-oth-er dream.
Glam-our trip so soon to slip. Eas-y come, but oh how quick it goes.

In de-mand, but sec-ond-hand, it's been heard
Sun-day's star is Mon-day's scar; out of date
Ten foot tall, but what a fall; hard to o-

be-fore you e-ven play.
be-fore you're e-ven seen.
pen yet so eas-y to close.

Up to date, but
At the top, so
Front page news, but

came too late. Bet-ter get your-self an-oth-er name.
quick to flop, you're so new but rot-ting in de-cay.
so a-bused. You just want to hide your-self a-way.

* To play along with recording, tune all strings down one whole-step.

You're so right but o - ver - night you're the one who has to take the blame.

Like but - ter - fly, so quick to die, but you're on - ly look - ing for to - day.

O - ver - paid, but soon you fade be-cause you're on - ly look - ing for to - day.

To Coda

Ev - 'ry - one just gets on top of you.

The pain be - gins to eat your pride.

You can't be - lieve in an - y - thing you knew.

When was the last time that you cried?

Yeah, yeah.

Figure 2 (2 bars)

Look - ing for to -

*D5 = D(omit third)

** This two-bar vocal pattern continues during Solo, but fades out after 14 bars.

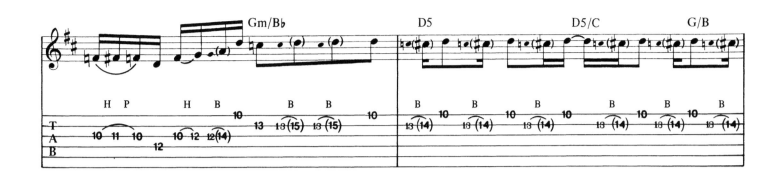

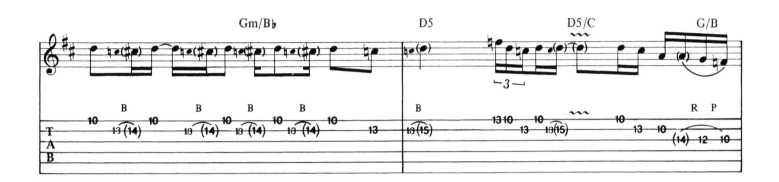

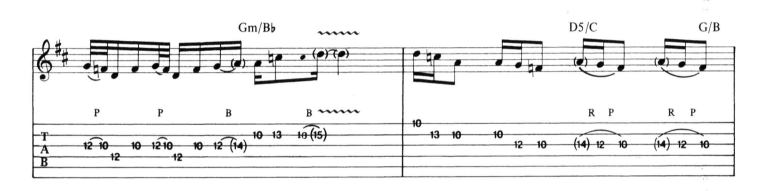

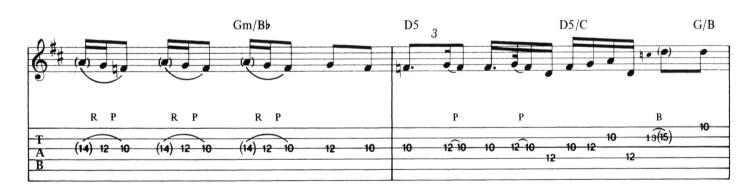

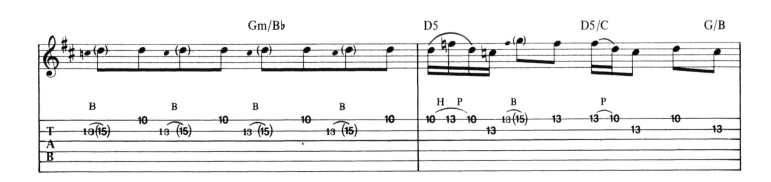

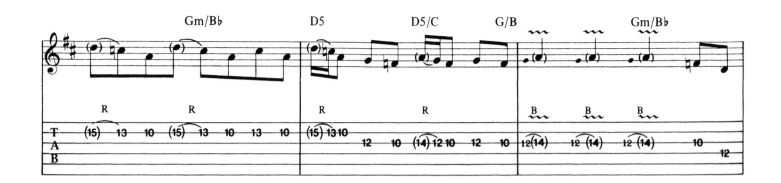

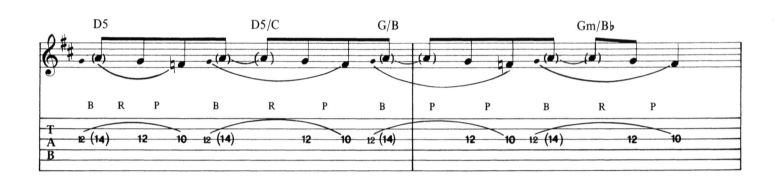

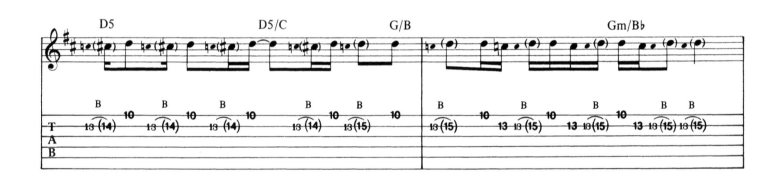

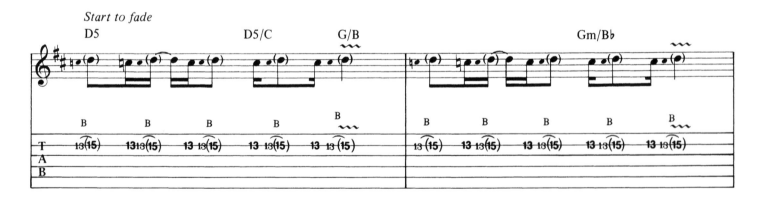

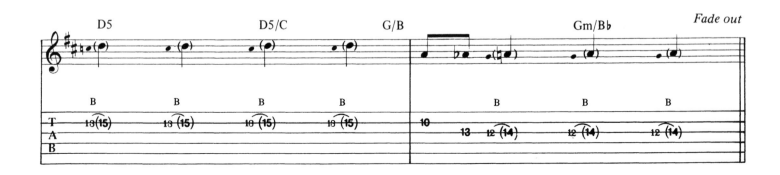

Fairies Wear Boots/Jack The Stripper

Words and Music by Frank Iommi, John Osbourne, William Ward, and Terence Butler

*Indicates note played by Bass Guitar only.

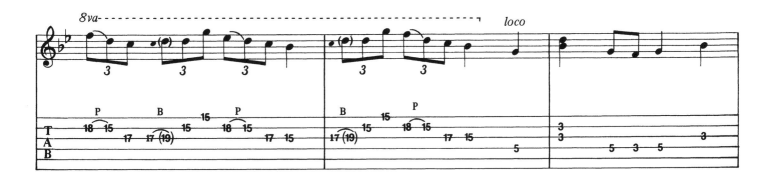

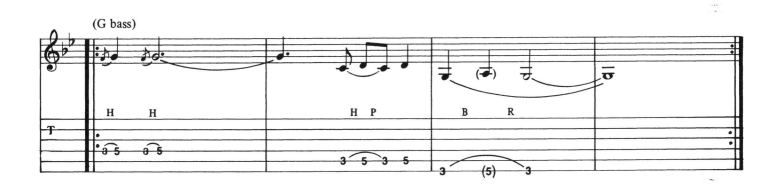

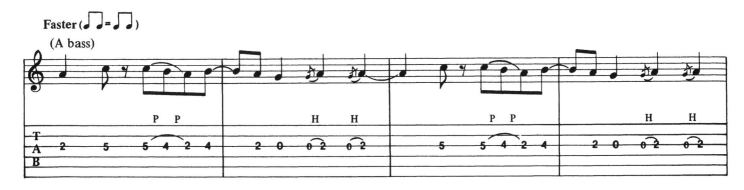

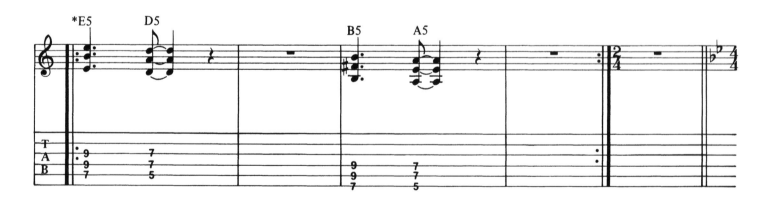

*E5 = E(omit 3rd)

Repeat and fade

Heaven And Hell

Words by Ronnie James Dio
Music by Ronnie James Dio, Terence Butler, Anthony Iommi, and William Ward

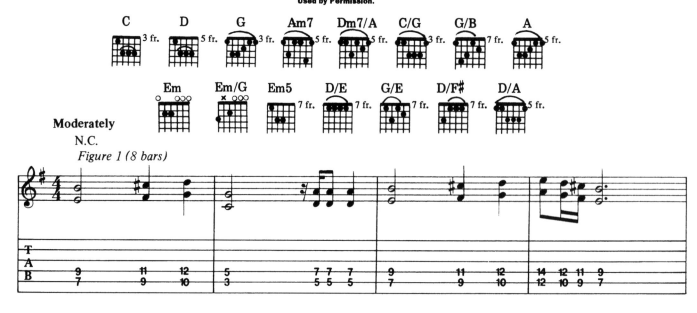

Moderately

N.C.

Figure 1 (8 bars)

Figure 2 (4 bars)
Bass part adapted for Guitar

Continue Fig. 2 for 8 bars

Sing me a song;___ you're a sing - er.
lov - er of life's___ not a sin - ner.
seems to be real,___ it's il - lu - sion. For ev - 'ry

Do me a wrong;___ you're a bring - er of e - vil. The
end - ing is just___ a be - gin - ner. The
mo - ment of truth___ there's con - fu - sion in life. ___

*Indicates note played by Bass Guitar only

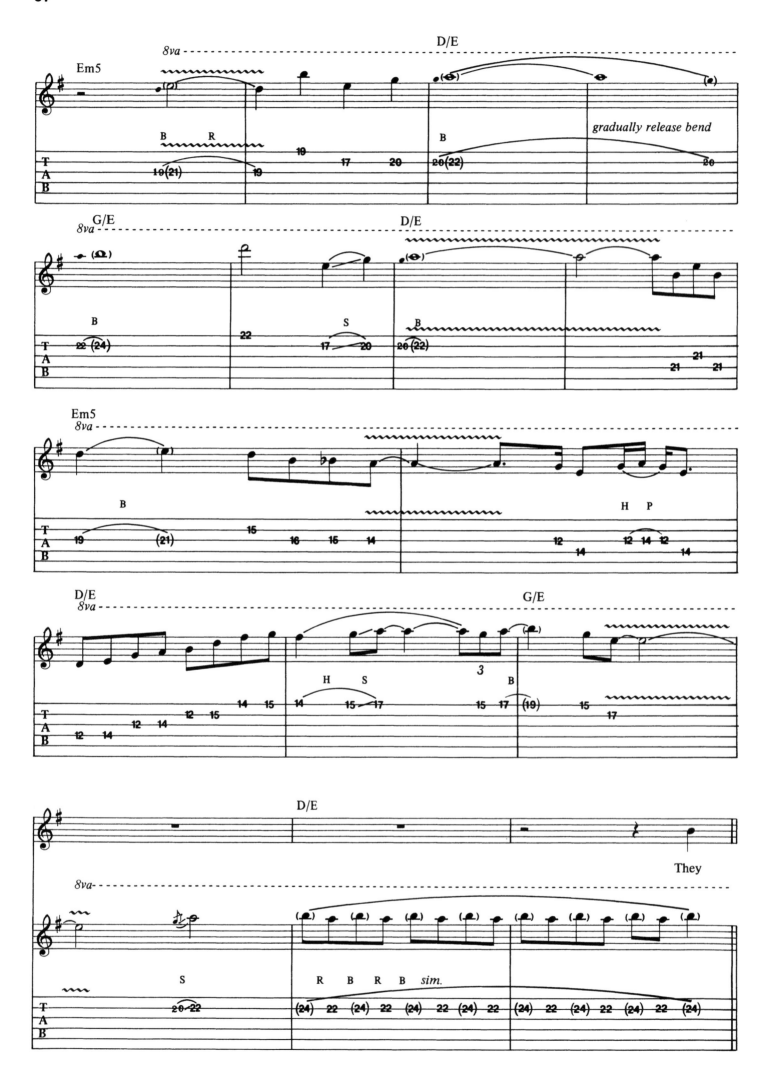

They

Iron Man

Words and Music by Frank Iommi, John Osbourne, William Ward, and Terence Butler

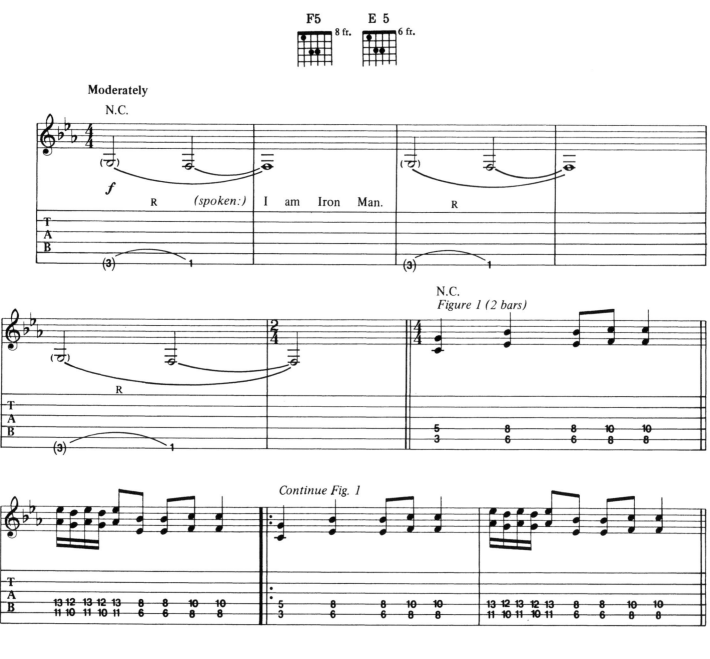

Can   he   walk   at   all   Or— if he moves,— will he fall?
We'll   just   pass   him   there.   Why— should we——— e - ven care?

Continue Fig. 2

P

6 5 6 5 6 5   6 6 8 8

1.2.   3.

3 3 3   1   3   2   1 1 1   0 1 1 2   1 1 1
                                    1

Play Fig. 1 for 4 bars.   *Play Fig. 2 for 4 bars*
4

He   was   turned to steel   in— the— great— mag-net-ic field
Now   the   time   is here   for— I-ron Man——— to spread fear.

Where   he   trav-eled time   for— the— fu-ture of man-kind.
Ven-   geance from the grave   kills— all the peo-ple he once saved.

*F5   Eb5   3

No-bod-y   wants— him.—   He just stares— at the
No-bod-y   wants— him.—   They just turn——— their

Figure 3 (2 bars)

10   8
8   6

*F5 = F(omit 3rd)

world.
heads.

Figure 4 (2 bars)

F5
Play Fig. 3

Eb5

Plan - ning his ven - geance
No - bod- y helps him.

that he will soon un -
Now he has his re -

N.C.
Play Fig. 4

1.
Play Fig. 1 for 4 bars

fold.
venge.

Double time
(♪=♩)

2.
(Continue Fig. 4)

Solo I
*(D bass)

H P   S   H   P   P H

* Indicates note played by Bass Guitar only

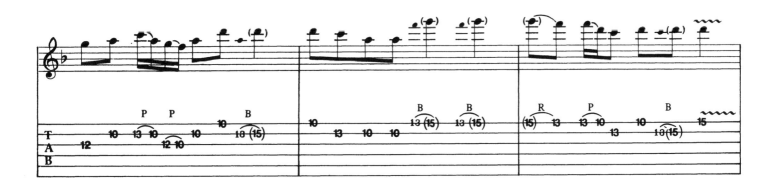

End of Solo

Tempo I

Play 4 times

40

Heav - y bolts of lead, fills_ his_ vic - tims full of dread.

Run - ning as fast as they can, I - ron_ Man_ lives a - gain.

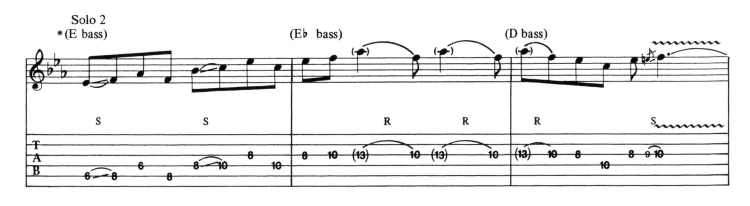

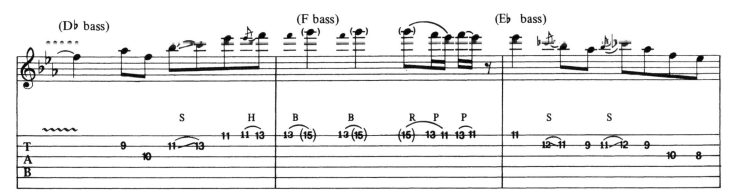

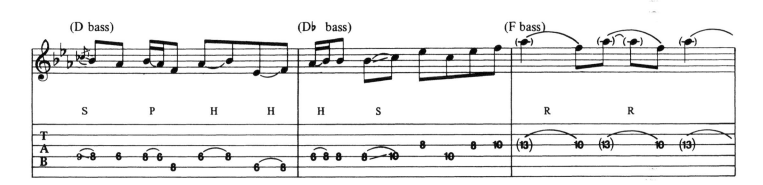

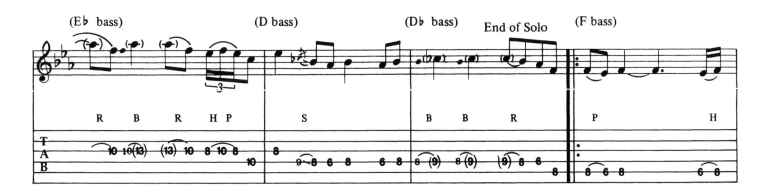

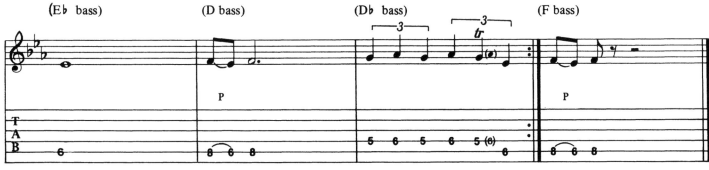

* Left channel overdub not notated

Play 3 times

N.J.B.

Words and Music by Frank Iommi, Terence Butler, William Ward, and John Osbourne

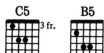

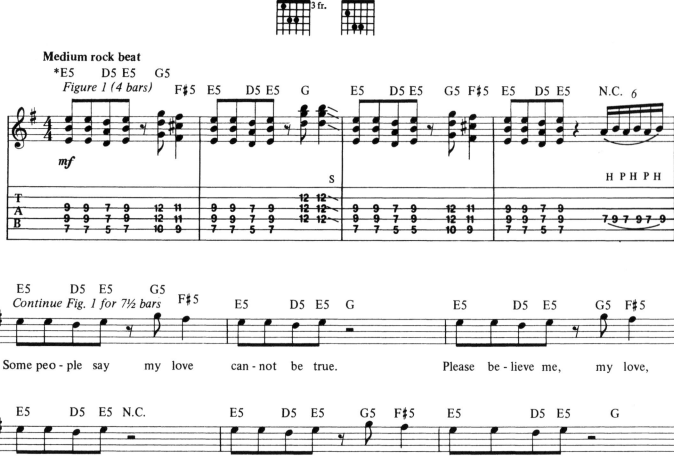

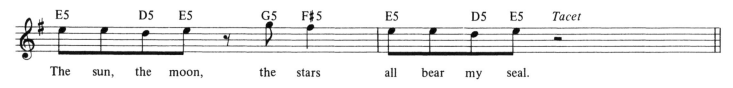

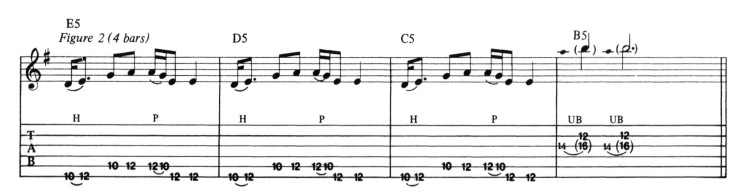

*E5=E(omit 3rd)

Fol - low me now and you will not re - gret living the life you led

be - fore we met. You are the first to have this love of mine

for - ev - er with me till the end of time. Your love for

me has just got to be real be - fore you know

the way I'm go - ing to feel, I'm go - ing to

feel, I'm go - ing to feel.

Now I have you with me un - der my pow'r. Our love grows strong - er now

with ev - 'ry hour. Look in - to my eyes; you'll see who I am. My name is Lu - ci - fer;

please take my hand.

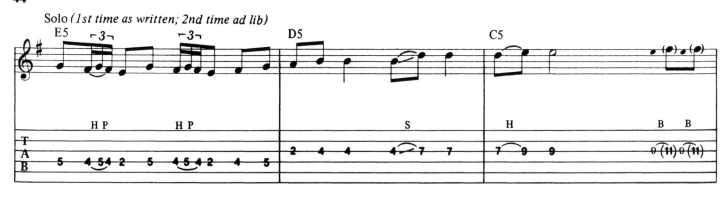

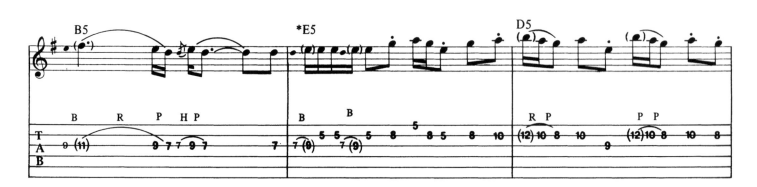

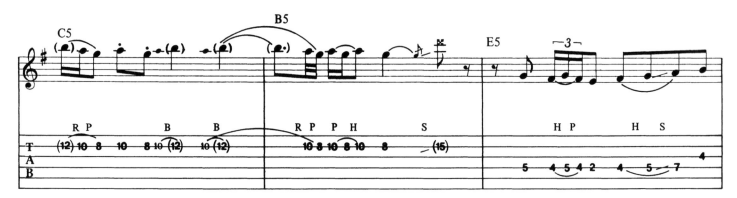

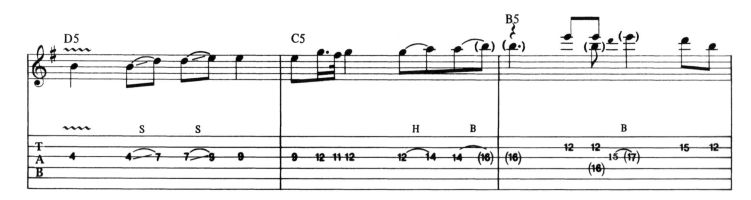

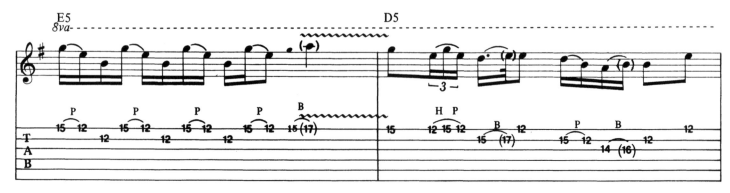

* Left channel overdub not notated.

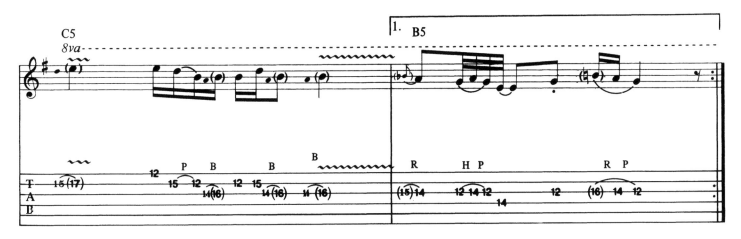

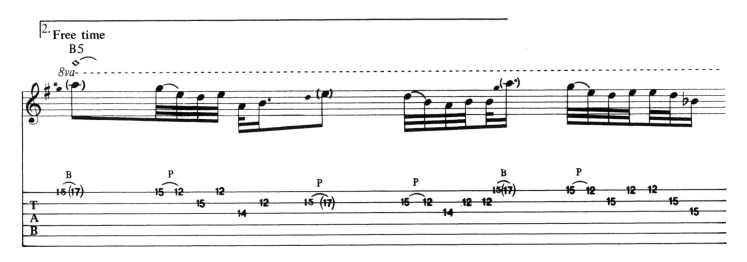

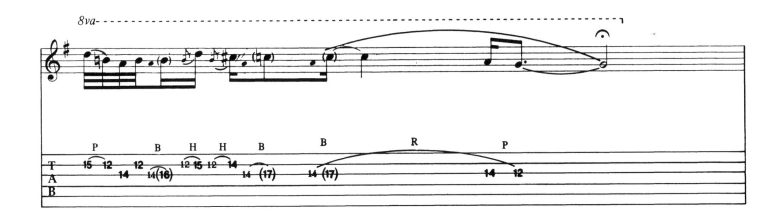

* Right channel overdub not notated

Never Say Die

Words and Music by Frank Iommi, Terence Butler, John Osbourne, and William Ward

1.2. Don't they ev - er have to wor - ry?
3. There's no need to have a rea - son.

Don't you ev - er won - der why?
There's no need to won - der why.

It's the part of me that tells you, oh,

*F5 = F (omit 3rd)

don't you ev - er, don't nev - er say die._____

Nev - er, nev - er, nev - er say die_____ a - gain.__

Play Fig. 1 *Play Fig. 3*

Some -

Don't you ev - er say die. Don't

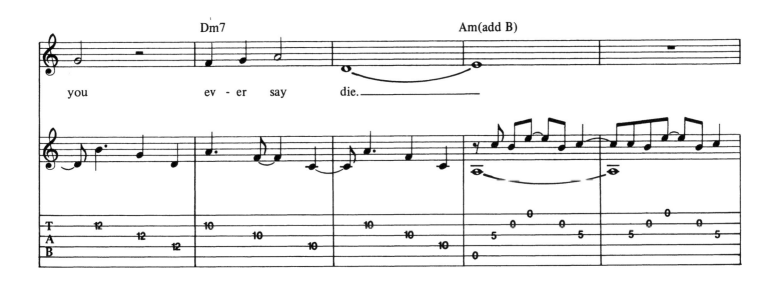

you ev - er say die. _____

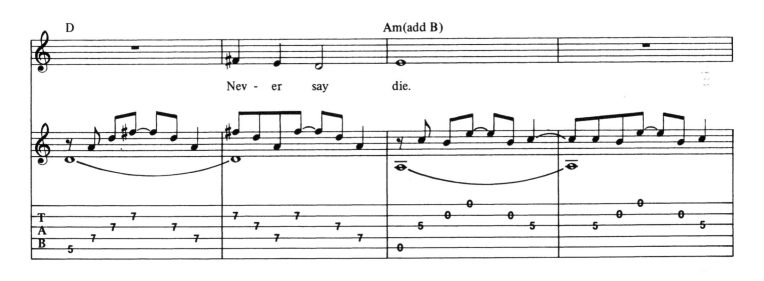

Nev - er say die.

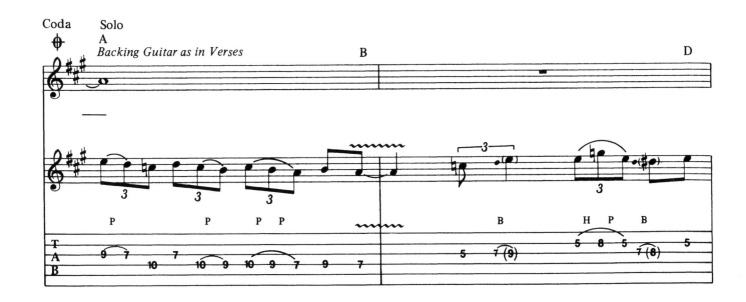

Nev - er say die.

A National Acrobat

Words and Music by Frank Iommi, William Ward, Terence Butler, and John Osbourne

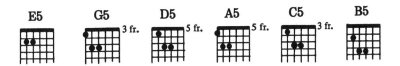

Moderately slow

Play 4 times

I am the world_ that hides_ the u - ni - ver - sal se - cret of all time.___
When lit - tle worlds_ col - lide,_ I'm trapped in - side_ my em - bry - on - ic cell,___

De - struc - tion of_ the emp - ty spac - es is my one and on - ly crime.__
And flash - ing mem - o - ries_ are cast in - to the nev - er - end - ing well.___

I've lived a thou - sand times.__ I found out what it means_ to be_ be - lieved.___
The name that scorns_ the face,_ the child that nev - er sees_ the cause_ of man,___

The thoughts and im - ag - es,_ the un - born child that nev - er was_ con - ceived.__
The death - ly dark - ness that_ be –

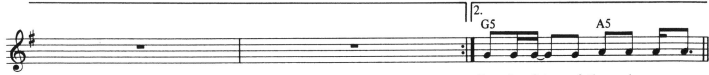

lies the fate_ of those who nev - er

*To play along with the recording, tune all the strings down one whole step.
**E5 = E(omit 3rd).

*Indicates note played by Bass Guitar only

Neon Knights

Words by Ronnie James Dio
Music by Ronnie James Dio, Terence Butler, Anthony Iommi and William Ward

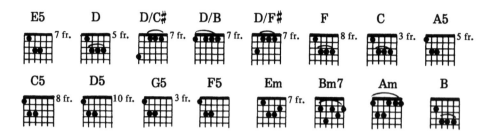

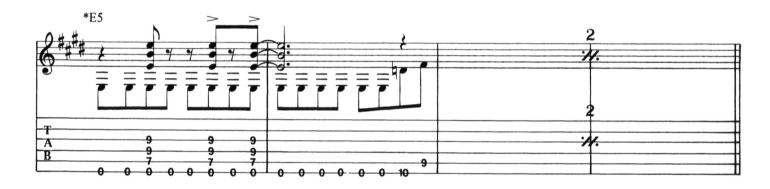

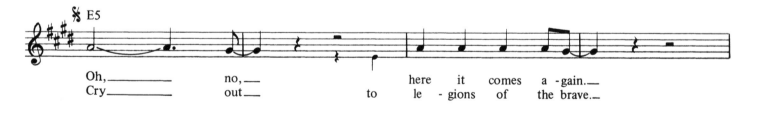

Oh,_____ no,_____ here it comes a-gain.____
Cry_____ out_____ to le - gions of the brave.____

Can't re - mem - ber when___ we came so close to love be -
Time a - gain___ to save___ us from the jack - als of the

fore.
street.   Hold on.____
                                     Ride out,____   pro -

*E5=E (omit 3rd)

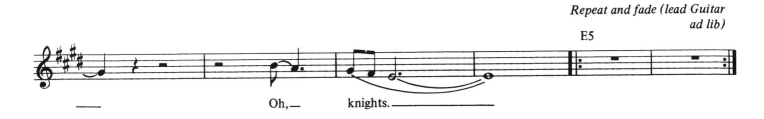

Repeat and fade (lead Guitar ad lib)

Paranoid

Words and Music by Anthony Iommi, John Osbourne, William Ward, and Terence Butler

* E5 = E (omit 3rd)

I need some-one to___ show me___ the things in life___ that
I can't see___ the things_ that make_ true hap-pi - ness.___ I

I can't find.

must be blind.

Solo

E5

Backing Gtr. plays Fig. 1 for 16 bars

Make a joke_ and I___ will sigh_ and you will laugh_ and I will cry.
Hap - pi - ness_ I can - not feel_ and love to me__ is

so un - real.

And so, as_ you hear_ these words_ tell - ing you now___ of my state,
I tell you_ to en - joy life.__ I wish I could,_but it's too late.

Sweet Leaf

Words and Music by Frank Iommi, John Osbourne, William Ward, and Terence Butler

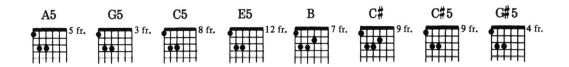

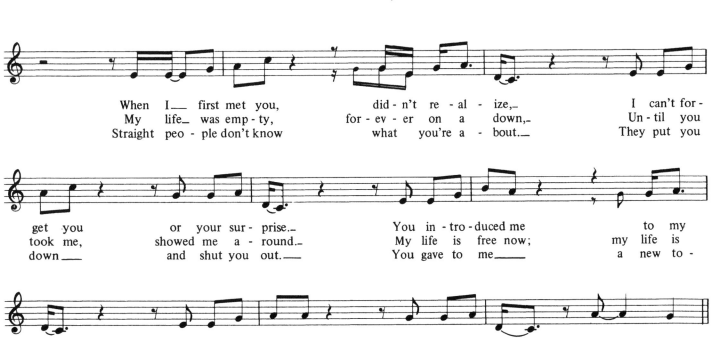

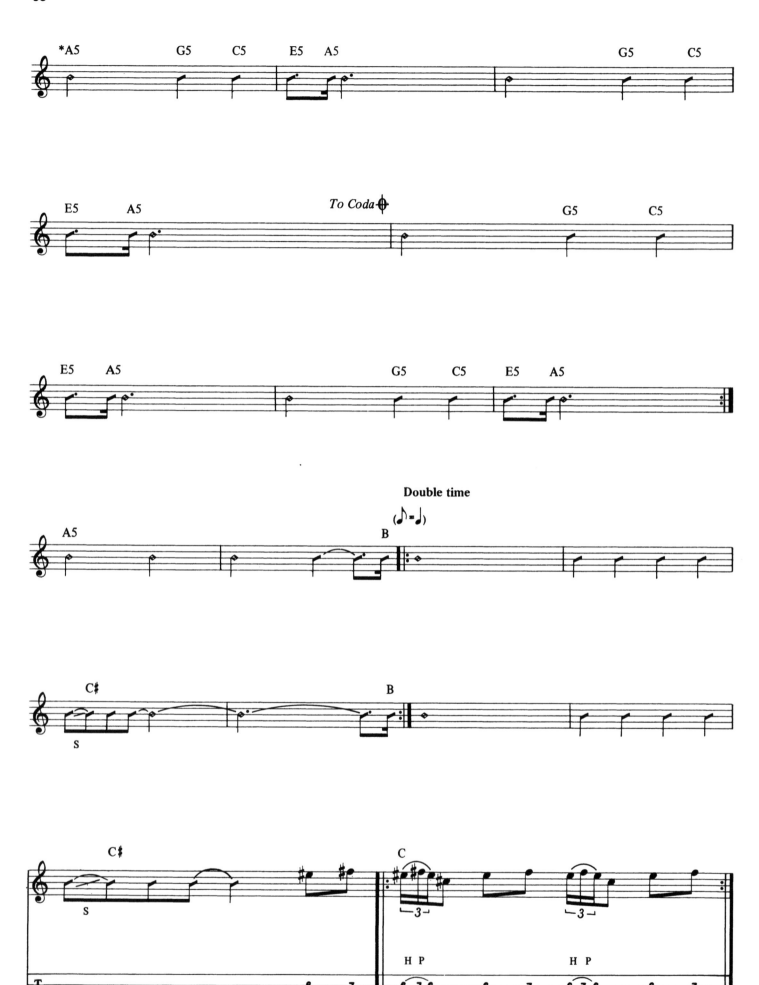

*A5 = A (omit 3rd)

Play 4 times

Play 4 times

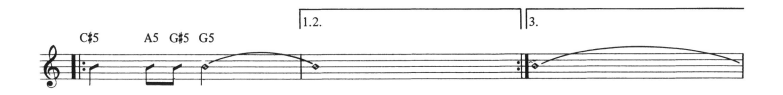

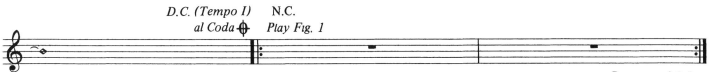

Repeat and fade

*Indicates note played by Bass Guitar only

Sabbath, Bloody Sabbath

Words and Music by Frank Iommi, John Osbourne, William Ward, and Terence Butler

*To play along with recording, tune all strings down one whole step.
**D5 = D(omit 3rd)

No - bod - y____ will ev - er let you__ know,_____

When you ask__ the rea - son why._____

They just tell__ you that you're on your__ own, ____

Fill your head__ all full of __ lies._____

You bas - tards!

Solo
Backing Gtr. plays Fig. 1 throughout

Where   can   you run___ to?
Ev - 'ry - thing   a - round___ you,

Sleeping Village/A Bit Of Finger

Words and Music by Frank Iommi, Terence Butler, William Ward, and John Osbourne

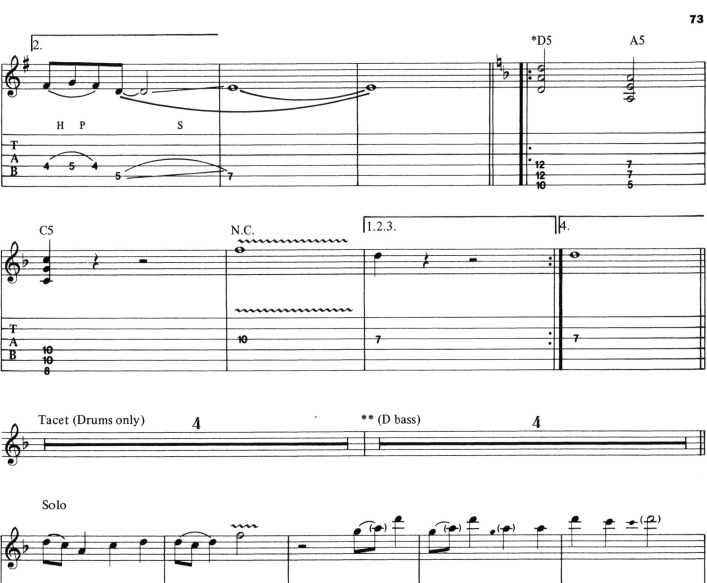

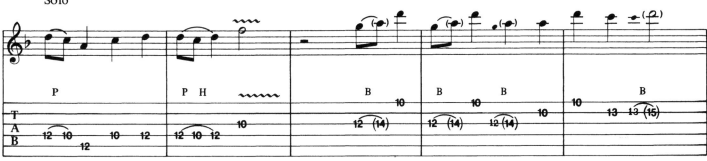

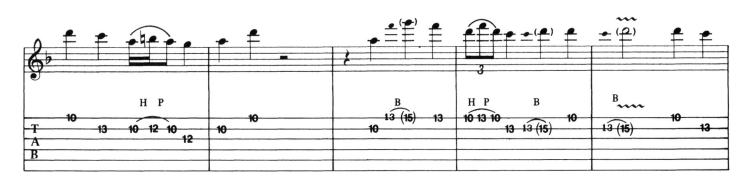

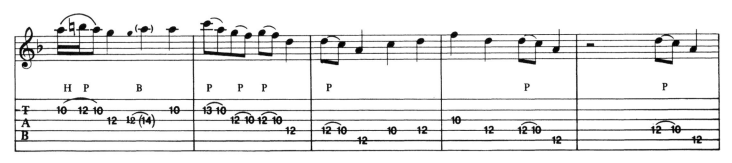

*D5 = D(omit 3rd)

** Indicates note played by Bass Guitar only

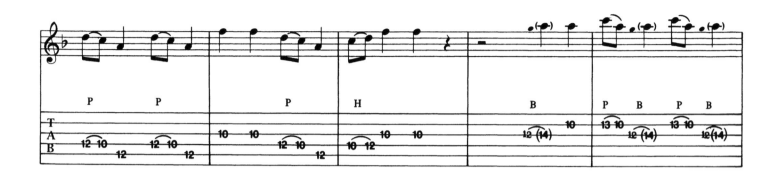

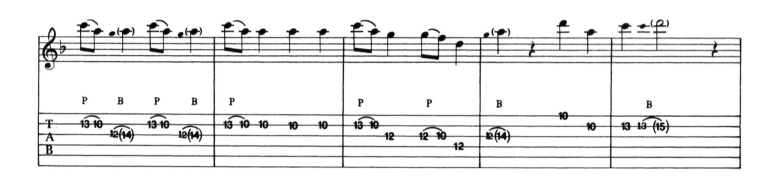

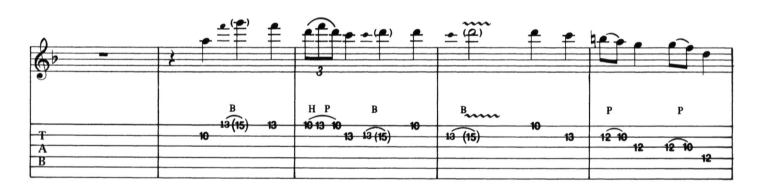

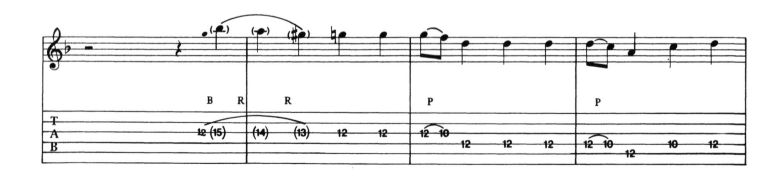

Snowblind

Words and Music by Frank Iommi, Terence Butler, William Ward, and John Osbourne

What you **get** and **what** you **see,**___ **things** that **don't** come **eas-** i - **ly.**___
Feel- ing **hap-** py **in** my **vein,**___ **i** - **ci** -**cles** are in my **brain.**___

Some- thing **blow-** ing **in** my **hair;**___
Death would **freeze** my **ver** - y **soul;**___

win- ter's **ice,** it **soon** was **dead.**___
makes me **hap-** py, **makes** me **cold.**___

*To play along with recording, tune all strings down one whole step.
**E5 = E (omit 3rd)

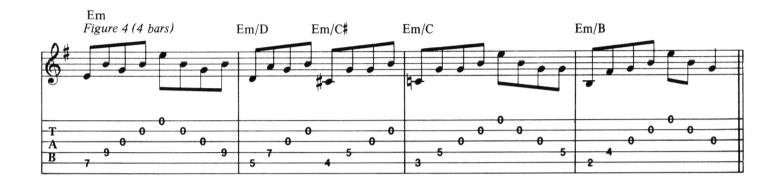

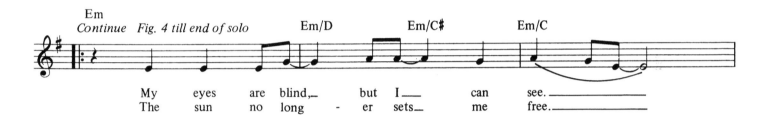

My eyes are blind, but I ___ can see. ___
The sun no long - er sets ___ me free. ___

The snow - flakes glis - ten on ___ the
I feel ___ there's no place freez - ing

1.
tree. ___

2.
me. ___

Solo

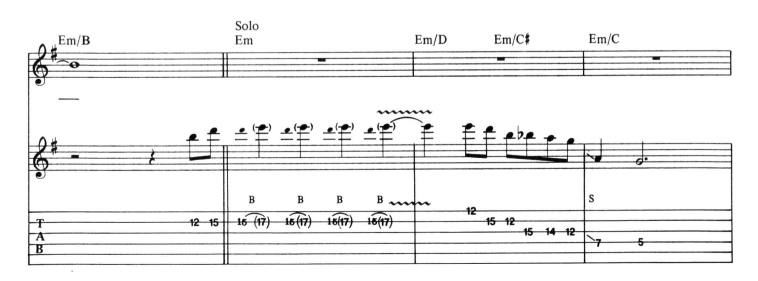

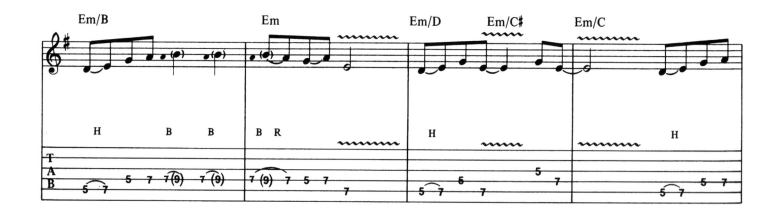

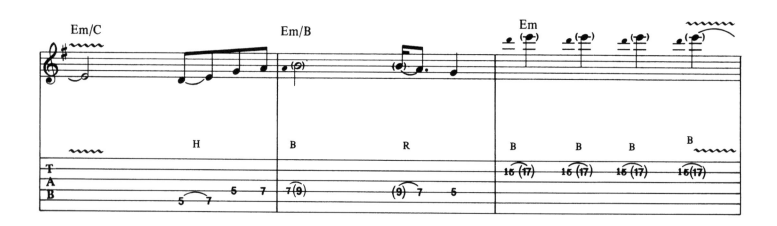

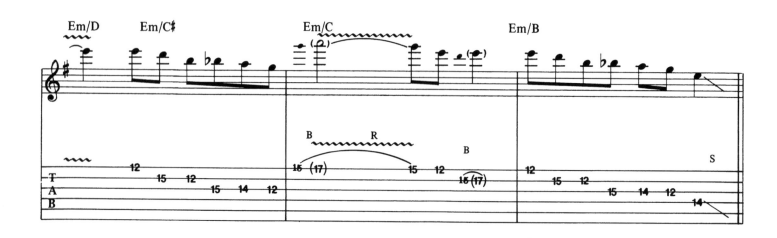

War Pigs

Words and Music by Frank Iommi, John Osbourne, William Ward, and Terence Butler

As the war__ ma - chine keeps turn - ing._____
On their knees__ the war pigs crawl - ing,_____

Death and ha - tred to man - kind,_____
Beg - ging mer - cies for their sins._____

Poi - son - ing__ their brain - washed minds._____ Oh, Lord, yeah.
Sa - tan, laugh - ing, spreads his wings._____ Oh, Lord, yeah.

Figure 2 (16 bars: 4+4+4+4) *G5

*G5 = G (omit 3rd)

Play 4 times

Solo I
*(E bass)

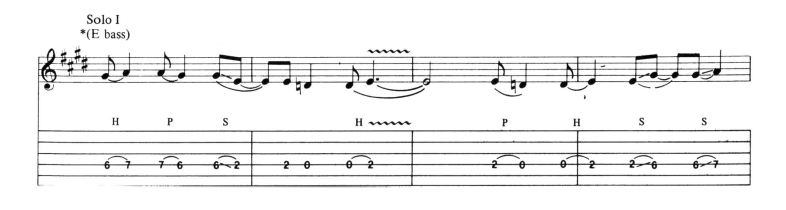

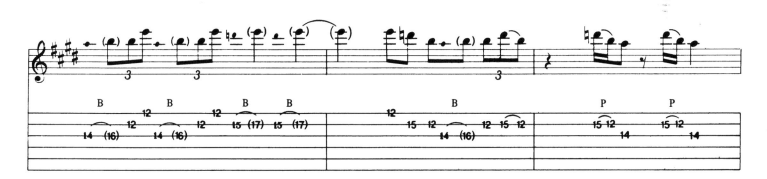

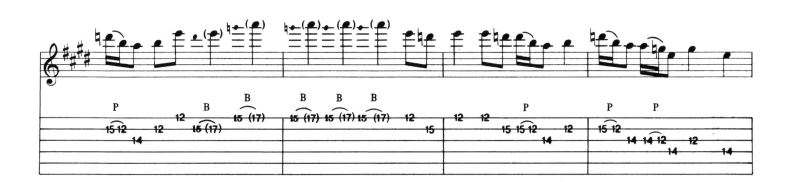

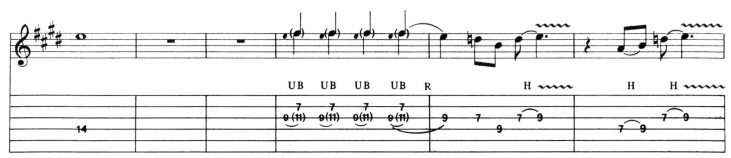

*Indicates note played by Bass Guitar only.

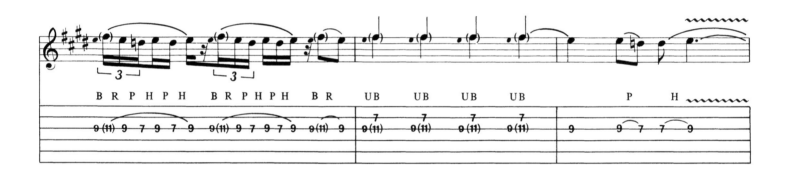

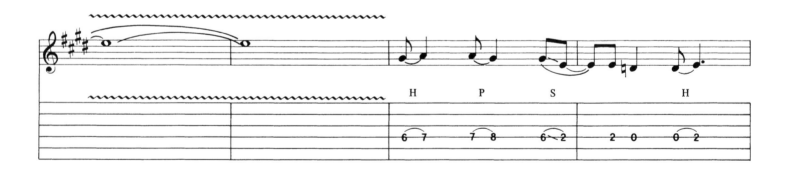

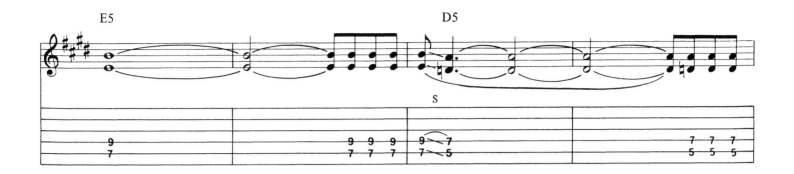

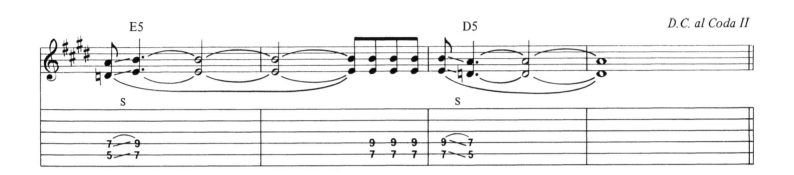

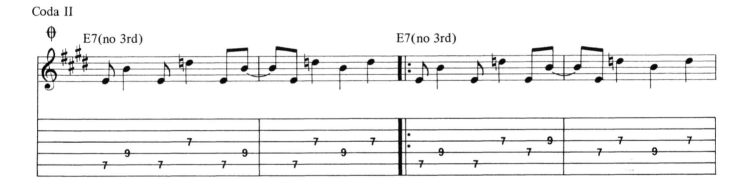

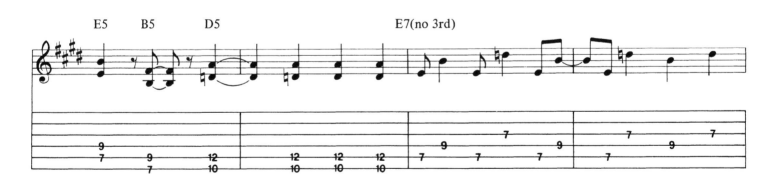

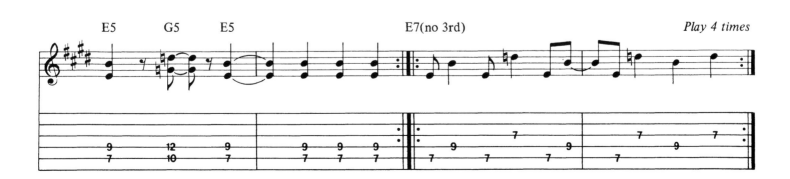

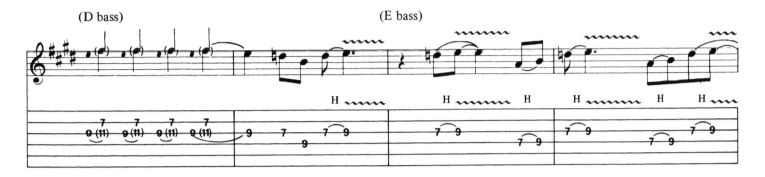

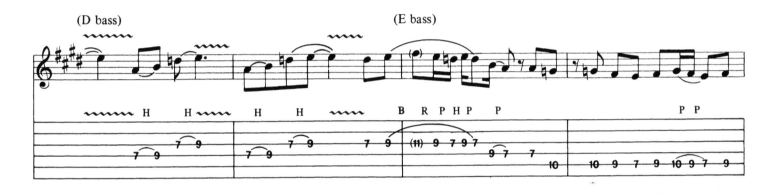

D. S. S. (with repeat) al Coda III

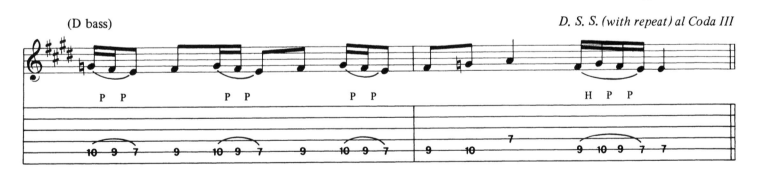

Coda III

Play 5 times (on 4th time, accel. till end)

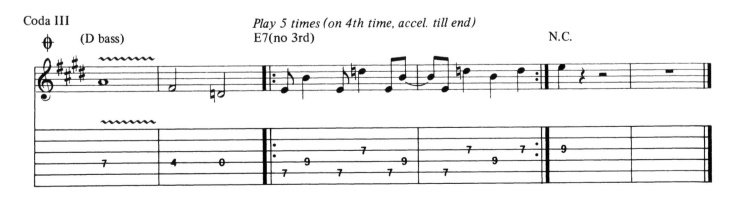

Symptom Of The Universe

Words and Music by Frank Iommi, John Osbourne, William Ward, and Terence Butler

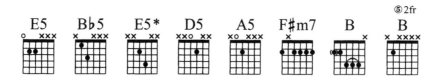

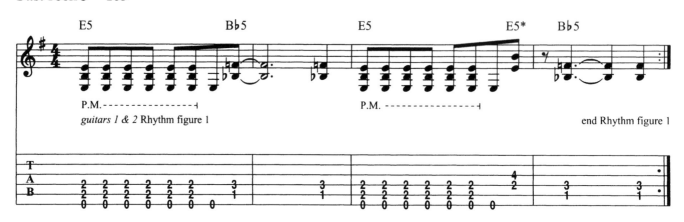

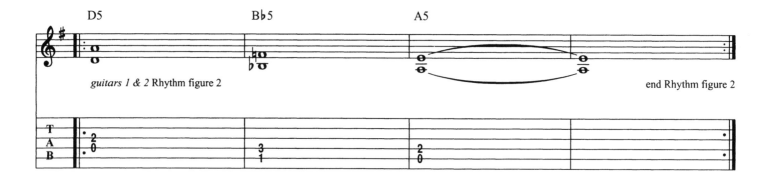

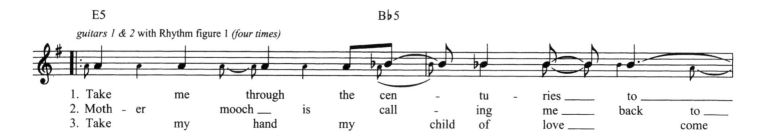

1. Take me through the cen - tu - ries ___ to ___
2. Moth - er mooch ___ is call - ing me ___ back to ___
3. Take my hand my child of love ___ come

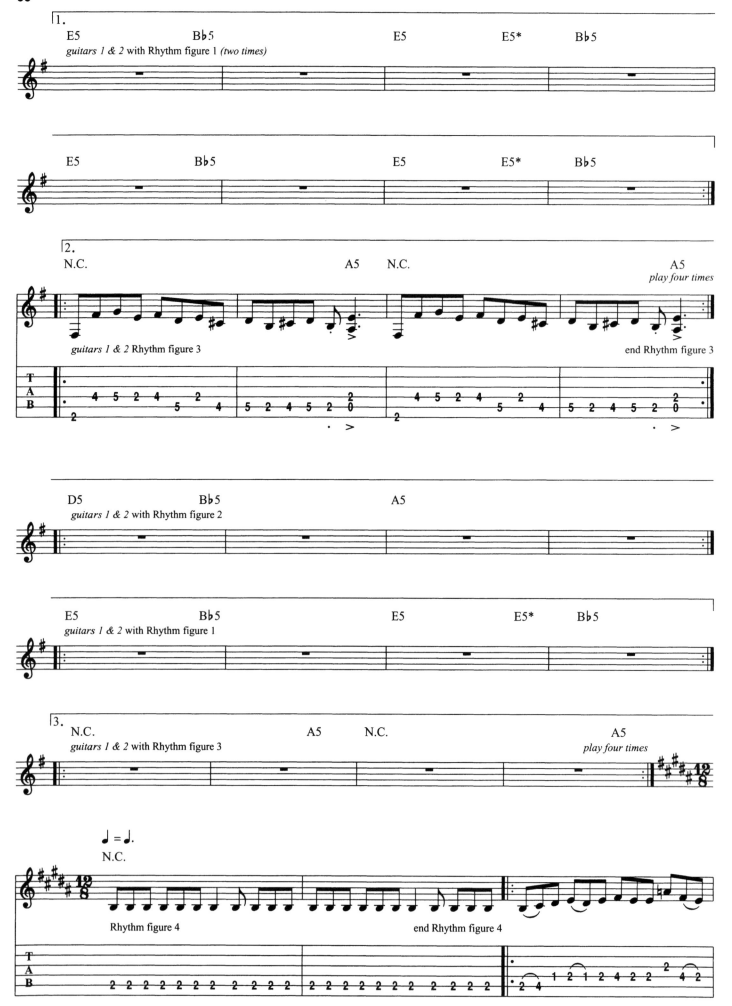

Guitar solo

A5

N.C.

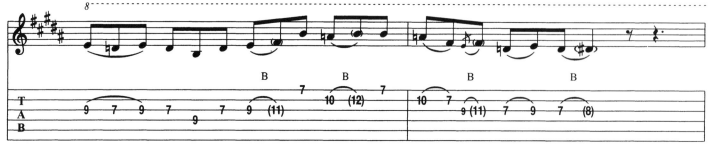

A5

⑤ 2fr

B

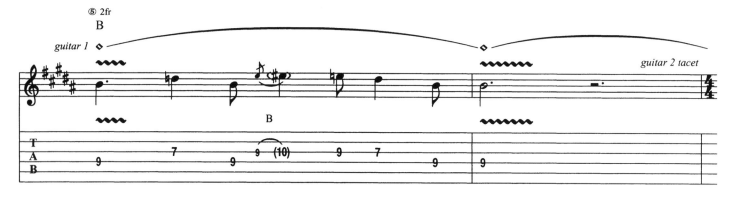

Slower ♩ = 84

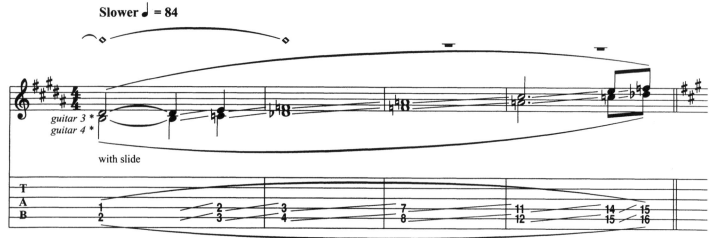

* Studio pitch shift arranged for two guitars

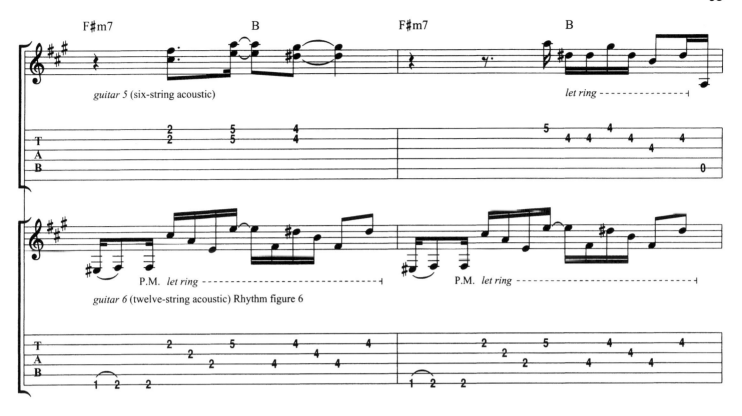

guitar 5 (six-string acoustic)

let ring

guitar 6 (twelve-string acoustic) Rhythm figure 6

P.M. *let ring*

4. Wom - an

end Rhythm figure 6

child of love's cre - a - tion _____ come and step in - side my

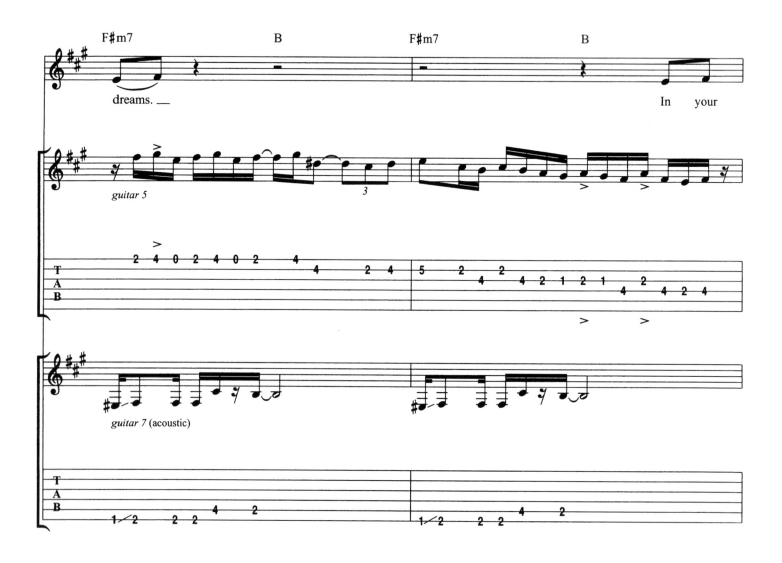

dreams. __ In your

eyes I see no sad - ness; _____ you are all that lov - in'

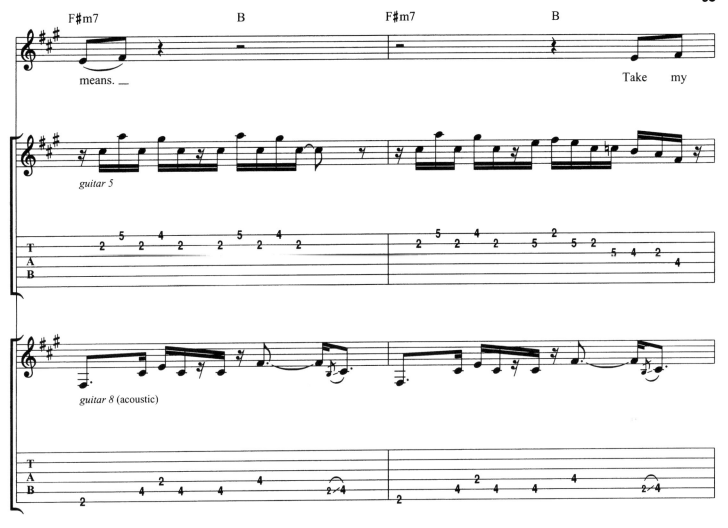

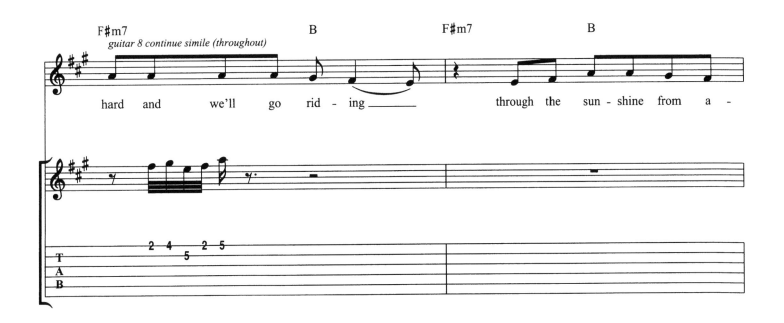

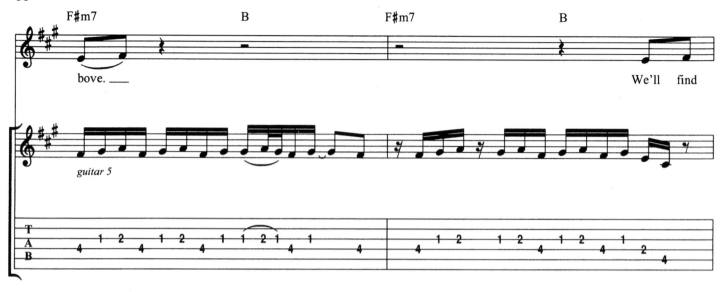

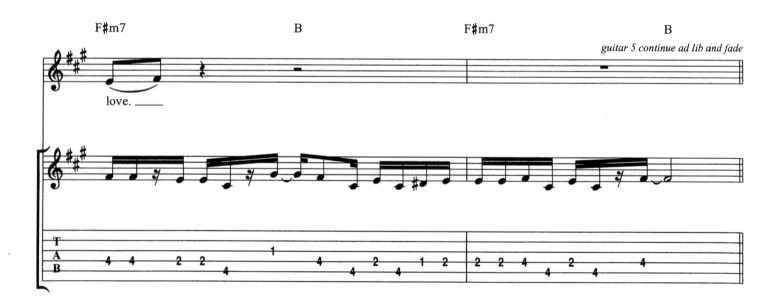